Agapi ke Thanatos
(Love and Death)

Maria Psanis

Moonlight Press
2003

Copyright©2003 Maria Psanis
All rights Reserved

No parts may be used, reproduced or duplicated
without permission of the author

Library of Congress Control Number: 2003090566

ISBN: 0-9707043-3-X

Cover Illustrated by Demetra Bakogiorgas

Poetry Books by Maria Psanis

- The Free Inhibited Child (1980)
- Thoughts, Love and You (1981)
- Immortal Shadows (1983)
- Today's Tears...Tomorrow's Laughter (1984)
- Searching For You (1989)
- Breaking the Cycle (1997)
- Asomatos Erotas (Bodiless Love) (2000)
- I Forgot to Ask God (2001)
- Agapi ke Thanatos (Love and Death) (2003)

Address all communications to:

Maria V. Psanis
2 Tunxis Road
P.O. Box 554
Simsbury, CT 06081

www.poetmaria.com

In loving memory of my Father
Vasilios E. Psanis

Contents

The Prayer of Saint Francis   ix
Help Me   9
Contemplate   10
Greek Song   11
Trust the Unknown   12
Archangels   13
Your Shadow   14
How?   15
Longing   16
Senses   17
God   18
Empty Spot   19
Your Cross   21
i Hear You   22
Accepting   23
Will to Live   24
Passing Away   25
Fire   26
A Prayer   27
i Give You   28
Blindly   30
Healing   31
Devotion   32
You Realized   33
Invite   34
Body and Soul   35
Invisible   36
His Child   37
Young Woman   38
Desire   39
One More Time   40
Humility   41
Don't   42
Wisdom   43
Agapi ke Thanatos (Love and Death)   44
In Harmony   45
Faith   46
Want To Be   47
Who Am i?   48
i Listened   49

His Presence   51
Enlightened   52
Spread   53
Letting Go   54
Invites Me   55
i Asked   56
Non-Believers   57
Confidence   58
For Centuries   59
Remember Me   60
Blessed   61
Peaceful Death   62
Unknown   63
Alone   64
Aching   65
Relationship with God   66
One Last Time   67
i Give to You   68
Emulate   69
Transforming   70
Interconnecting   71
Roaming   72
Goodbyes   73
Death   74
Gifts of God   75
God's Plan   76
Hungry   78
Love   79
Borrowed Time   80
Focused   81
i Walk   82
Memory   83
Unspoken Words   84
Expanding Borders   85
Enigma   86
To Liberate   87
Your Death   88
Your Eternity   89
For i Must Live   90
Dressed in Black   91
Until   92
Coping   93

The Prayer of Saint Francis

Lord, make me an instrument of your peace.
Where there is hatred let me sow love,
Where there is injury let me sow pardon,
Where there is doubt, faith,
Where there is despair, hope,
Where there is darkness, light,
And where there is sadness, joy.

O Divine Master,
Grant that I may not seek so much to be consoled as to console,
To be understood as to understand,
To be loved as to love.

For it is giving that we receive,
It is in forgiving that we are forgiven,
And it is in dying that we are born to eternal life.

Help Me

Are you listening God?
My painful plea.....

Hear me!

Take the pain
Free the body
From deadly disease.

Restore the heart
Unlock the soul
Demolish wrong paths.....

i am your angel,
your servent,
your ambassador -----

Are you listening God?

Help me to help
your creation
to die without
aches and wounds.

Teach me to sow
your love, your strength.

Erase fear from
the dying sick.

Who says death
is the end?

Oh!
my tears, a joy!

i hear you
God!
Eternity.

Contemplate

i feel your fear
Don't be afraid

Rest your hurting body
upon my faith

Your loneliness a storm,
your pains weeds and thorns.

Rest your affectionate glance
upon my optimism.

Let go!
Hear your High call

Free your soul
Contemplate God's home----

Rest your wounds
upon my palms

Your spirit blossoms
a new Spring
on my Winter's woes.

Greek Song

You walked the earth
with joy and pain
Danced an authentic
Greek song
with pride and courage.

Without guilt
unable to settle
with this or that
Safety wasn't your name.

Your heart filled with fire
Adventure rested
inside your veins
Didn't dwell in your limitations

You took charge
tempting to accept
archangel Michael as your Friend
A prayer…
…boundless love…

At peace
at last.

Trust the Unknown

God's heart
is your home,
You live in Him.

Look and act
like Him.
Fill yourself
with Love.

Don't fear death,
it's only a new
beginning that has
no end.

Trust the unknown.
Free yourself
from earthy comforts.

Detach people
from your soul.

Walk alone…
Heaven's door wide open.

Archangels

The archangels sent by God
to take your soul,
Don't fear
Don't frown.

Kiss cosmos
one more time,
Softly whisper your goodbyes.

The end,
a beginning,
No tear,
No struggle,
No pain.

Among the stars
you're the brighter one.

Your light
a trail of hope.

God takes care
your soul.

Your Shadow

Behind me
your shadow follows…
without a doubt----

Your wrinkled face,
crippled walk,
wither body,
Fights
for one more breath,
a tighter caress,
a drop of love,
a kiss, a touch.

Neglect you not.

Your audacity,
i hear,
Ask God to
take you home
Forgive your wrongs.

Your wounded body
is buried
under the sun,
there's no storm.

The cross no longer
yours.

Your soul transparent
as a gentle breeze

the battle ceased.

You have learned
the power of Love.

Now you're dancing
in the arms of God.

How?

i prayed
for God to
take you home

Your sickness
a sharp pain
in my heart and soul.

How do i let go?

You've been with me
endless years.

You taught me
to say what i mean,
to act without fear,
to stand tall no
matter what,
to fight for justice,
And hold no grudge.

i prayed
for God to
take you home.

How do i let go?

Your footprints left behind
an open road
for my guide.

i hear the screaming wind
the silent storm
And in your eternal sleep
i rest my woes.

We shall meet again
my dearest heart,
the debt is paid
with signs and blood.

Longing

Longing to touch your eyes
with my glance
i look ... i face God.----

His blood,
wreath of thorns,
nails,
a cross.

For you and me
the world to
repent of wrong,
Regret...

Longing to hear your voice
with my heart
i hear ... heaven's lyre.

No clouds,
No rain,
No gate keeps me away.

Your soul plays
with me
with open arms i feel ...

You're Free
to dance, to sing.

Senses

Your heaven
connects my earth to you.

Waterfall your silence
inside my soul.

i see you're wrapped
inside the arms of God,
Nightingales sing your songs.

Your body wither
with aging years.
Your spirit young
like a butterfly,
Flower to flower
to take and give.

You left behind
a Legacy.

i feel no pain,
i have no tears,

You touch my world daily
with rainbow colors
only i see,

feel,
touch,
hear.---

Your heaven
connects my earth to you.

Oneness.

God

i hear my sister cry
"Why Daddy did you have to die?"

My brother's sighs and tears
Leave a painful trail in my being.

Why are we born
if we're going to die?
i hear a voice from inside.

God wants us to learn
to accept each other
for who we are
with an open heart,
Not to be stingy with our love.

Material possessions, fame,
power and greed
shouldn't come first.
The naked spirit is worth
much more.

No one should be
above the one below.

United we become
one soul.

God.

Empty Spot

Without clinging
to your cross,

i watch you
casting your fears,

relaxing in the arms
of Death,

waiting for God's hand.

i kissed your
tired face
with love
and gave you permission
to fly far.

You smiled and said
yes
while my sister
held your hand.

She cried and cried
and wouldn't let go
even when
the doctor told her so.

My brother prayed
for God to come
and take your soul,

Mother wasn't able
to see you go,
she hid behind
a concrete wall.

Oh! Daddy
your empty spot
We fill it with
enormous love.

Your body is no longer
with us
but you travel gently
in our hearts.

Your Cross

You walk alone
touching lives
with truth and love.

No matter what
tomorrow brings,
You live each day
with courage,
hospitality
compassion
without fury and fear.

You houseclean your spirit
before you speak,
listen to the movements
of your words.

You don't close your eyes
in despair.
You reach out
embrace humanity.

You carry civilizations inside
your dreams.

On the road to Calvary
You bare your cross
with pride and bravery.

Your body is crucified,
but not your soul.

i Hear You

Emotionally involved
with you,

i dare to love you
beyond the end.

i am aware, your human
body died,

immortal your spirit
flies high.

i sat with you
at your deathbed,

cried and whispered my
farewell.

There's no distances
to keep me far

i hear you
with my ears of heart.

Accepting

Flashes of your whole life
before your eyes
searching for meaning…

Silently accepting your death.

Consciously feeling my touch
your eyes communicating
not holding on.

Resting your thoughts
on my heart's rhythm
i hear your fear.

Caressing your face
with my lips
you smiled.

Endlessly you spoke
of the place you were born,
childhood years,
wars.

i cried.

Will to Live

You never contemplated
your death –
There was always
a tomorrow.

You were in control.
You danced life.

Even when you where
spitting blood
Denied
the end was near.

Refused to leave
the physical world.

Yet when angels came
to take you home,
you saw the light,
willingly you left your body.

Entering a new beginning,
embracing the unknown,
your smile remained behind.

Passing Away

Angels watched over you...
...for many years.
Until a cure was not
to be...

God reached out His arms
and whispered
"Time to come to me"
And told the angels
"set aside, this man is mine."

Slowly passing away
i could not
stop or make you stay.

A courageous heart
no longer beats,
your generous hands
rest in peace.

Memories of you
give me strength.
Now i dance
your unfinished dance.

Fire

Do i have to?

A volcano erupts
from within.

Fire melts my being.

i have to!

God has
my heart His.

A Prayer

You're with me, God
i know.

i see you in every step
i take,
hear you in every sound
i hear,
i feel your presence wherever
i look
i touch your love with all
i speak,
inside your hands
my sins dissolves.

Obedient to you
i kneel,
i pray.

i glorify your name.

i Give You

Haven't you learned
not to wallow in guilt.
Confronting your games
brings inner peace.

i give you my heart,
hold my hand,
Understand.

Haven't you learned
underneath your façade
hides a child who seeks
kindness and love.

i give you my wisdom
take my works
Freedom calls.

Haven't you learned
to dance with the wind
Embracing a thunder
raises our wonder.

i give you my faith
my light to see
walk your path
without fear.

Haven't you learned
your partnership with God
He will never abandon
your broken heart.

i give you my surrender
so you can find strength
reach, seek, find yourself.

Haven't you learned
to face your truth
Harboring bitterness
imprisons your soul.

i give you my addiction
to pure love
Place yourself
in steps of God.

Haven't you learned
not to be afraid of life
Reverting to self betrayal
cripples your flight.

i give you my unconditional devotion
Open your heart!

The Holy Spirit
will feed you
with divine love.

Blindly

God takes wrong
and makes it right.

He responds
to our callings.

Don't tell Him and
not do.

Vividly i feel Him.

When i lose
track of Him,

i find Him.
strength in my weakness,
Love in my anger.

i do not question,
i do not seek.

i trust His
existence, blindly.
He's in my heart eternity.

Healing

Giving up attachments
in silence.

Healing God's world
with compassion
and kindness.

Love channels
spontaneous
accomplishments.
Inspires my vision.

Disciplining
the mind,
the body healthy

Keeps the Spirit
eternally free.

Devotion

i drink love
from the cup
God serves me.

With open heart,
i sing
my intimacy
with Him

i feel His arms
around my soul
His kisses, raindrops
on my thoughts

i dance and dance
and my senses
half drunk, half alert
in His Beloved image
i grow.

i turn to God
whom i trust,
intoxicated, thirsty,
For his divine love.

My devotion
enhances
His undying Love.

You Realized

Death opened a door
into the presence of God.

Taking residence in His home
you observed your
home you left behind.

Your body was sheltered
but not your Soul…

A tear, a whisper
a deeper breath,
a cry. ---

The price was extravagant
you realized.

Burdening yourself
with this and that
Rules were a cross you carried

Bruised, with a wounded heart
endured the pain.

Thirsty in your quest
you rose above your past

Heaven invited your heart
to rest
in God's Kingdom.

Seeked forgiveness
Repent.

Invite

Don't give up…
Trust…
Believe…

Have Faith!

Invite God
to be your passion.

Heaven on Earth.

Body and Soul

The body
mud and soil
one with earth.

The spirit
energy and love
one with God.

Invisible

Are you aware of my presence?
God asked
Do not bargain
to see me, to believe

I'm invisible
like the oxygen you breath
like the wind you feel
Either you have me
in your heart or
neglect my existence.

No matter how you use me
I'm Love.
I'm the creator
Believe it
or not.

Are you aware of my presence?
God asked.

i closed my eyes
in the darkness

i felt His touch.
Light.

Wholeness.

His Child

i worship God
for giving me
more than
i have given.

i am His servant.

Young Woman

"God loves you"
this strange young woman
turned and said to me.

She smiled
and walked away.

"i love Him too"
I whispered
behind her
not knowing her face
nor name.

It felt as if
an angel dropped
in front of me
with whom God
sent this message.

No broken self
No bitterness.
No hurt.
No pain.

Renewal.

Desire

A burning desire…
… God …
i climb the highest mountains
i struggle in the deepest
clear blue seas.

My soul searching …
…seeking …
to give myself
with knowledge
and holiness.

My prayers …
… not from the head …
i see.
i feel.

My heart open river
my silence a desert
isolated, perplexed.

Setting free my sins …
… naked …
my umbilical cord connected
to the Universe.

With opens arms …
.. touching skies …
Spiritually free
healing wounds.

A burning desire …
… Death …
Renewal.

One More Time

i weep
in silence.
No eye can see
my sorrow.

i hide my face
in your immortality,
my pain
manifests tears.

The Holy Spirit
dwells in my soul.

i feel
your paradise.

My lonely heart
aches
to touch your face,
one more time,

to hear your voice
one more time,

to kiss,
to hug
you,
one more time.

i weep
in silence.
No ear can hear
my thunder.

Humility

My love for God
bigger,
greater,
than any love.

My soul sees,
feels,
turns to Him.

He wipes
away
my sorrow
my tear.

He follows
my footsteps,
Holds me
not to
crumble.

Chases the moaning
the pain.

With a pure mind
Humility
turns me humble

The servant, i,
in peace
and love.

Don't

Don't criticize,
Don't hate,
Don't have your way,
don't hold onto anger.

Don't seek to conquer,
Don't have control,
Don't dress with power,
Don't put on a façade.

Desire nothing.

Submit yourself
to the will of God.

You'll have everything.

Wisdom

Create …
Balance …
Detach …

Tolerate …
Accept …
Forgive …

Understand,
Experience.

Listen …
Insight …

No doubt.
One with God.

Agapi ke Thanatos
(Love and Death)

Clothed in His Agapi
rested his shame and guilt –
Confessed his sins.

Obedient he kneeled
without secrets he prayed,
worshipping His touch.

No longer hurting,
No longer broken,
he fixed his glance on God.

Escaping his genes
embracing His grace
he smiled.
Inviting Him
into his heart. ---

Down to his knees,
feeling God's agapi.

Flawless
giving himself to Thanatos.

In Harmony

You reside in my heart
i see you in my
memory
traveling like a gypsy
without a destination
kicking your fears
up in the air.

Body and soul separated
letting structure go
embracing change
bonding with a
spiritual glow.

i reside in your open valley
connecting to light and
laughter.

Your soul with my soul
creating a blissful
pathway.

Uniting
love and joy
in harmony with pain.

Faith

i contain the uncontainable,
the mystery,
as i travel across oceans,
engaging with cosmic quest,
embarking on the unknown.

Without control,
without fear,
without comfort,

Unlimited

Faith, my intimate lover,
invites dreams and hopes
to cultivate my passion
to an exuberant
dance in virtue and balance.

I contain the uncontainable,
the truth,
as i walk across valleys
my soul one with God
enduring tears and pain.

Want To Be

i don't want to be
you, God.
i just want to be
your shadow.

Who Am i?

Who am i?

What is my purpose?
What is the
meaning of my life?

Hiding in this and that
Longing for meaning.

Without God
i realize
i'm a nothing.

Career doesn't fill me,
Material possessions
have no value.

Sitting … observing
i worship my silence.

i feel Him running
through me.

i am love.

i Listened

Dropping my heavy burdens
on His lap
i listened to His
gentle whisper and
humble heart.

Moments,
hours,
months,
years.

i listened,
Questioning.

Resting my soul on His
wind and rain.

i asked for His blessings
to help those who suffer.

He gives me
Love to feed
the hungry,
the orphans,
the wounded
the lonely.

Moments,
hours,
months,
years.

i listened,
Seeking.

His thorns,
my headaches,
His blood
my tears,
His pains
my compassion.

i listened
sensing His call.

i am walking
His walk.

His Presence

My heart wide open,
my arms stretched out
hugging the Universe.

My soul, strong,
embracing darkness.

Without reservations
i pray in silence
surrendering my weakness
on His strength.

Speaking to Him
i cling to His love.

My eyes see emptiness,
my ears hear solitude.

My heart filled
with His presence.

Simple in humility
i feel God everywhere.

Temptations ceased.

Enlightened

With generous heart,
giving hands,
acknowledging God's light.

Hungry for solitude
passing no judgment,

My tongue rests in silence.

Deaf and mute
enlightened by His touch.

With open soul
allowing Him
to use me …

… being His tool
the self blossoms a new.

Surrendering to His plan
chosen to work for Him.

His love and compassion
dissolves my darkness.

Spread

Stop doubting …
walk with a daring step,
fearless.

Throw your mask.

Conquer your labels
with courage and perseverance.

Spread your love
in everything you see
and touch.

Empty your flame
inside darkness.

Watch your soul glow.

Freedom.

Letting Go

Don't hold so tight
Don't be a slave
to your own fears ---

Motivate freedom
by letting go.

Dance with an open
spiritual heart and
a clean pure mind.

Don't possess a thing.
Feed your soul
with duty and devotion.

Don't be afraid,
confess your darkness.

Without a scream
Don't seek the easy way,
Walk your Calvary
with pride and courage.

Your path engraves
Heaven and earth.

Invites Me

God works through me
He invites me
inside His heart
and dreams.

Child like innocence
with trust
i allow myself
to hear and feel,
His pains and aches.

My desires without
a human form.
Reveal to Him
my devotion.

Obedient to His path
He fulfills my wishes.

i Asked

i asked for His blessings,
He gave me His goodness,
and dressed me with Love.

Non-Believers

My motives
are to serve God,
with a whole heart
and free spirit.

My vision
one with His
i sacrifice
for the opportunity
to serve the non-believers.

i know Him, intimately,
He has given me
passion and faith
to touch His world.

i depend on Him.
He leads,
i follow.

Fearless i risk
my safety and security.
i gain courage
i mount up, i pray.

Confidence

My silent heart
hears my conscience
passing through me.

Thirsty to serve,
to give,
to help,
to rescue.

Fearless, stepping
on obstacles,
trusting the truth.

Having confidence
in God
i sail on open seas,
climbed the highest mountains,

to serve,
to give,
to help,
to rescue.

For Centuries

Without boundaries
Unlimited
Renewing
every moment.

Every hour,
every month,
every year.

For Centuries

i come and go
live and die.

Separating my soul
from my body.

Again and again
ruled by a
higher vision.

Preaching
God's love.

Remember Me

I hear your wailing
I see your tears,
I feel your stress.

I fight to stay but
my time is up.

Oh! my children
Don't worry
Let me go …

My soul will take me
where I belong.

Don't morn over my
ill body
it's my cocoon
I leave behind.

Witness the smile,
on my face
as I die …

Remember me!
But please
don't cry.

Dance my songs,
I leave behind.

Until we meet again
on the other side.

Don't stop …
… continue on
with life.

Remember me!
But please
don't cry.

Blessed

Enlightened by God's touch
i co-create His rhythm
Blessed,
Purified of my imperfection
my darkness evaporate.

Passionate for His light
i am
transformed into
energy and matter.

Holy the air i breathe
Miracle the earth, i walk

Healed from a polluted ego
the conscious influenced by
awareness and transformation.

Unattached
my soul
simple and poor
endowed in His power
i give to Cosmo
an innocent heart
without thorns and nettle.

Peaceful Death

You guide yourself
with the help of God.

Tranquil,

your spirit
rests quietly in Him.

Submitting your desires
in His light

Your strength,
Renewed.

Your suffering
no longer painful.

i loved your eyes,
your smile mesmerized
my dreams.

i gave to you.
my purity,
my tenderness
my greater love.
And carried your burdens
for countless season.

Hungry for love
you shared your dance.

i took you hand in mine.

A peaceful death.
i cried.

Unknown

Again and again
i pray to God,
with humble mind and spirit.

My powers, invisible,
fired with love
i feel His grace.

Simple words
run from my heart.

Without rehearsals,
without demands,

My prayer unknown
to Man.

Tenderness and compassion
overflows from my soul,
for All.

Alone

i am a shepherd,
Alone,
tending to the endless
meadows.
Bare feet
stepping on rocks and holes.

My emptiness
filled with God's grace.

Standing in front of Him
with an open heart,
and free spirit,
confessing my sins.

He wipes my tears
He softens my pains

Trusting His touch
i consult my desires.

No matter where i look
what i touch
My truth
His love.

Aching

An army of angels,
one by one
in silence walk
by my side,
as i tread softly upon seasons.

Aching to be
in company with God,
my solitary prayer
searching to hear
His speech,
to capture His glance.

In peace with Him
i hear His song,
i feel His tenderness
embracing love.

Ah! how sweet
our rendezvous
serenade and laughter
overwhelmed with passion
i sail my soul
against raged waves
with God i forget my woes.

Faith and courage
Holds my heart and hand.

Relationship with God

Guided by the highest
principles,
my connection with God
intimate and clear.

With a dreamy voice
i whisper my dreams
and fears.

Mindful,
with an open heart,
invisible grace
revealing my hidden pathos.

My mask unfolds,
cultivating my
relationship with God.

i give Him my insecurities,
my pains,
He gives me His friendship,
Listens to unspoken
words of the heart.

Entering the deeper
realms of my being,
in touch with my feelings.

One Last Time

My soul in peace,
watching you
as you travel
to say your last
goodbyes.

My hand on your shoulder
i pray for God
to let me feel your glance,
one last time.

To hug and kiss
your face
with my silent tears,
my aching breath
one last time.

Wrapped in solitude
memories traverses my heart,
bridging your heaven
with my earth

As i pray for God
to let me hear your voice,
to dance your passion
one last time.

You closed your eyes
i whispered i love you
in your ear.

Your lips, a smile,
For the last time.

i Give to You

i give to you
my devotion,
my truth,
my love.

i give to you
my darkness,
my sins,
my aches.

i give to you
my confusion,
my anger,
my despair.

i thank you
for filling me
with forgiveness
understanding,
compassion.

i thank you
for holding my hand,
for guiding me with light
for whispering
gentleness and tenderness
in my heart.

i give to you my life.

Emulate

i communicate with God,
i tell Him my fears.
He dwells in me,
fills me with Faith.

i trust His whispers,
i obey His teachings,
i emulate His behavior.

Transforming

Have you figured out
who you are?

Why are you here?

Harvesting life's meaning,
Reflecting.

Silently
in solitude,
in the arms of death,
you realized
a material world
you're leaving behind.

In an altered
state of consciousness
you recognized

the puzzle no longer in pieces.
Transforming your fear
into grace.

Your metamorphosis
angel wings.
You're flying free.

Interconnecting

Spontaneity
pulls beauty from within

Walking the journey
interconnecting my faith
with His love.

Consecrated to God
giving every breath
to you who's dying.

Dedicated to His work
Balancing my holiness
with simplicity and love.

My human cry surrenders
to pain and joy.

Thirsty to serve
the unservable.

A silent prayer
purifies my heart and soul.

You're finally resting
in the arms of God.

Roaming

i listen to You
with clean heart,
open mind,

My soul nurtured,
a gift from You
pure and free.

Empty with silence
i hear your presence
roaming within me.

Contemplating …
Reflecting …
Penetrated
i surrender myself in You.

Without a doubt
my child-like Spirit
invites you to play,

to take and use me
as you wish.
You're in charge
of my life.
My faith comprehends
your love.

i give to You
my world.

Goodbyes

You lied feet away
from material life
you were leaving behind ---

Reaching out i kissed
your fear
and whispered in your ear,
"i love you, Daddy,
don't be afraid
God is waiting
to take you home."

i couldn't understand
your response
but your eyes tender
and sweet
Looked around to see
Mother, brother,
sister and me.

Your grandchildren, angels,
around your bed
They didn't want you to
feel alone
as you were getting ready
to depart from your
earthy home.

It wasn't easy to say
our goodbyes,
in our hearts a void
you left behind.

Death

Don't be afraid to die.

You're going home
where you belong.
To be united with God.

To give your heart
and soul to Him.

Death, a higher step
to eternal life.

A paradise.

Gifts of God

i reach, i touch, i feel,
i hear, i see, i taste. ---

Joyful is the moment.

In harmony
with God's light. ---

My heart filled
with His love,
truth and humility.

i give to Him
whatever He wants,
i take whatever gifts
He gives me.

He gives me more
than i could ever dream
of giving.

My soul wrapped
in faith and truth
my every breath i breathe
For Him,
my every step i take
For Him,
my every dream is filled
By Him.

Balanced.

God's Plan

i told God my plans
He listened,
smiled and walked
away. ---

"Where are you going?"
vehemently, I asked
and ran after Him.
"Did you not hear
my plans?"

"I heard you my child,"
he stated
paused in silence,
He remained.

"Well, what do you think?"
i said
blocking His way.

"Oh! your plans
are not my plans,"
with apologetic tone
He voiced.

"What do you mean,
i don't understand
this is all my choice"
i voiced.

"Yes, it is,"
He softly expressed.
"But my plans for you
differ from yours,
and touched my being
with His light."

Suddenly i obeyed.

"I'm yours"
i softly whispered
and made Him dance.

My plans, His plans.

"United we stand"
i sang …
celebrating our dance
together.

Hungry

Hopeless,
lonely,
angry,

Suffering,
pain,
despair,

Hungry
for Love.

Without
expectations.

Love

Sacrifice
your need.

Live without
that
you cannot do
without.

Love.

Borrowed Time

Standing in front of you
my heart wrapped in tears and pain.

i want to cry
i want to fight,
Yet in silence i remain.

i look at you in your deathbed
my mind swifts
to a life you leave behind.

Oh! How can it be?
time to return
your earthy key.

i understand
we are only here
on borrowed time,

God wants you
on the other side.

i see your eyes filled with fear,
i feel your heart without a beat –
my tears tip-toed inside your soul.

Focused

i pray …
      i wait …
           i trust

i fear …
      i have faith …

           i keep focused.

i speak to God

      embracing grace.

i Walk

i dare to dream
with passion and enthusiasm

Without competing
Looking up
see what He sees.

Faith demolishes fear.

Yearning to be meek,
merciful,
peacemaker, pure in heart.

i shift my attitude
creating
a vision of heaven ---

Allowing the Holy Spirit
to dance in me

i walk with Jesus.

Memory

i long to know
if you're safe in Heaven.

i close my eyes
to see beyond the earth.

You come wind, rain,
your dawn, dew
on my rainbow soul.

i reach out,
i touch air,
Your breath
caressing my
four clover heart.

A bitter-sweet memory
travels in my glance.
You come and go
Free from earthy comforts.

A sharp pain,
a tear,
a smile

Missing you …

Unspoken Words

My aching heart cries
the unspoken words
as i watch
leaving your body.

Your soul rised.

i trust the Lord,
you're free from pain.

Your hand
in my hand.

Fearless
your crossed
the other side.

i let go,
i cried.

in my dreams
you come
and go ---
Revealing your
paradise home.

Expanding Borders

Because i love
i sacrifice

God works through me.

i depend on Him.
Fearless
Embracing Truth.

i jump my comfort zone
expanding borders.

i watch God
doing His work.

Willingly i allow Him
to use me ---

Faith conquers
my limitations

A new horizon
unfolds my soul.

Enigma

Spring
born an innocent child,

Summer,
young, strong
dreams to conquer.

Fall,
wise, content
Peaceful with
rainbow colors.

Winter
old, wrinkled,
Fading in the arms
of death.

Until Spring,
Reborn
to live, to die,

Enigma

To Liberate

Oh! Lord
Your blessings
my strength,
my vision.

Humble
i seek
to balance
my inadequacies,
to liberate my pain,

to embrace Your grace,

You serve me miracles ...

Your Death

   Your death
       transforms
             my pain
into poetry ...

Your Eternity

i embrace your galaxy.

A star nests
inside my eyelids.

A howl nourishes
my voice.

Lightning pulls sobs
out of me.

Your eternity
forces me
to confront
your absence.

For i Must Live

Silence
contemplates
your voyage with me.

i cannot follow
your path.

Not now.

For i must live
life so i can
keep you alive.

Dressed in Black

Sadness holds my hand.
Vulnerable,
my tears, an ocean,
bring me memories
and dreams,
laughter and joy.

My eyes hold
a solitary wind,
inviting you
in my thoughts.
Seizing your dance,
my heart dressed in black
morns your finished song.

Until

i invite you
to stay for awhile
until my tears
no longer fog my eyes.
Until my pain
no longer twists my heart.
Until my words,
no longer dig my soul.
i invite you
to stay for awhile.
Until my abyss
no longer numbs my speech.
Until my sadness
no longer tumbles my steps.
Until my vigilance
no longer bow and arrows my grief.
i invite you
to stay for awhile.
Until i learn to celebrate your life,
not dwell in your death.
i invite you
to stay for awhile.

Coping

Coping with your death
i realize in every tear
there's a new day,
a new dream,
a new sunrise,
a new moonlight,
a new beginning ...